Whispers of Eternity

Kartik Ahuja

BookLeaf Publishing
India | USA | UK

Presentation by *BookLeaf Publishing*

Web: www.bookleafpub.com

E-mail: info@bookleafpub.com

ISBN: 9789363309647

First edition 2024

To my king in the making, equally talkative as Me, my son Shaurya Ahuja

ACKNOWLEDGEMENT

Firstly, my 11th-class English teacher Mr. E.T Mani who gave an assignment for poem writing.
Next my Professional communication teacher, Bonny Pannu Ma'am, who listened to my poems and offered encouragement.
Continuing, my friends who were my initial audience and critics.
My Family: my parents, my wife, my lovely brother and my bhabhi, who heard me and probably sometimes got bored as well.
My holistic coach Shriya Agarwal who gave me a lot of encouragement and feedback as well.
My open mic super audience where the crowd cheered for me with no judgment.
My rejections in love and friendships that pushed me more towards poetry, and lastly to the people who recently decided to part ways, claiming I meant a lot to them but perhaps, not that much.

Disclaimer

PREFACE

As people resonate with the various feelings that they have in mind, it may seem so causal and similar but still may be different in the poetry.
My thoughts bring my life and its associated phases in simple words. You may find it like it was written by a child as it doesn't have the great big word flavor but think once while reading, as if you are imagining a movie scene, and then decide if you want to read the second poem.
Beauty always lies in the eye of the beholder. Think about yourself when you read each poem.

Attachments for the love

We fought and we cried, life was different together,
It is different alone as well,
The beauty was in the smaller moments, that we spent together,
The beauty was in the video calls that caused our love forever,
The beauty was in the distance we had, but still the attachment prevailed,
The beauty was in the jealousy that we both had and that we could not end this tale,
The beauty was in those eyes that always refused to accept my love,
The beauty was in you when you stood in front of me like a dream came true,
The beauty was talking with no barriers in front of me, with no video screen,
It all changed slowly and gradually, when I saw you in tears and the reason was me,

The element each day was becoming worse as I failed to understand,
What caused you to make this distance so big and an abrupt one,
My mind froze for a few days and then electrical charges just crippled my body,
All the beauty now remains in ruins, as you distance yourself away,
Crippling my heart slowly to say, my mind is so weak it can hardly translate,
I am just angry all the time, with you not around to support is what I can say,
My love for you was pure, although many obstacles stayed, I lost you in this life to say,
Maybe I want you back, but still it's hurting a lot my attachment to you was spiritual,
As it was from miles apart, I want to wish you the best for celebrations in life,
I am still jealous and selfish a lot, maybe in some life we can be together, hold hands and finish what we started together,
All I can now want is a quiet sleep leaving my soul as the attachment for love is deep,
Hope I meet you in the afterlife where the beauty of those eyes shines brighter.

Darkness Your Cuddle is Different

Darkness, your cuddle is different, it is a simple acceptance from me that you are around,
You feel no different, as you are not haunting but the breaths of people are haunting you,
You are quiet and listen to the noises that people make and still have no complains,
To cuddle you and sleep is a kind of rest that I feel is needed but, I still wake up at night to see when you will pass by me,
While people may enjoy the sunrise and the redness of the sky, but I most certainly see the same when you come like the moon and stars to light the sky,
Darkness, your cuddle is love in my lonely life as you hear my voice and make no judgment of

my feelings at last, I have a friend like that for always,
Darkness, your cuddle is different, and your love is pure that is all I can see.

Tired Of Pain

I am sleeping but don't feel that I am asleep,
I hurt so much but still choose not to show the hurt,
I am lost but still choose to guide others in the shining light of my wisdom,
I am depressed but I still choose to smile every now and then,
I think I am over you but still love you so much,
I think I don't miss you, but still every second, think about our old conversations,
I think I hate you, want revenge, and dream of misery and pain for you but still want to help resolve all your life issues,
I don't talk to you but still feel that you are always around whenever I close my eyes,

I want to slowly drift away into dreams of you
but feel that then I will miss seeing you one
more time,
I think I have no pain but still I am tired of the
pain that hurts me all the time
I think that I am expandable, heartbroken,
betrayed, humiliated, and tired of pain but still I
wake up to hope, happiness, be included and
think you will come back

Drop

I am not an end to a sentence,
I am not an end to an alphabet,
I am not a Circle drawn and colored,
But I am a mistaken ink carelessly spilled,
I am a spoiler of the page and a non-associated entity,
An element from which people run away or discard freely,
No alphabet wants to be next to me, they start after 2 lines,
I wonder why I am so alone in the dark,
Finding those answers, I am sitting in the garbage, crumbled as if I'm an old scar,
I know wounds heal, and they say the difficult times will pass,
Still, I feel someday if I am included with a thought that would bring new life to this unknown corpse,
I will also live with purpose and not stop; I will no longer be a Blackstar.

Tears

I may be water that is just salty but I help take away the pain,
I may be inexpensive but still worth a hug and a small joy away,
I may appear in the eyes but still fill up in the heart,
I may be of happiness or sorrow but still present with all once in life,
I feel bad for those who can't cry, as I am tears which just come from the eyes, whether in pain or joy,
Hidden in the rain or just left free, I am present in all situations, and you can easily find me,
I can be considered beautiful or scary,
life is unpredictable and will bring so much to you; I am just one part that you didn't know,
Tears, Tears, and Tears roll down your cheeks; I am simple, don't complicate me.

Favorite

It's a beautiful feeling to remember the time
when I was refreshed from my sorrowful mind,
Stress, issues, and problems are not what best I
can handle, as I am hardly breathing as a
survivor,
Expectations are always so high, that it becomes
a burden for me,
I can hardly walk my path with all the heaviness
that is upon me,
Bad luck moves around me, with troubles as if
both are my best friends,
I am lost in this thick fog, barely able to see my
hand, thinking about where my path is to go,
Then suddenly I hear your voice, which seems to
be very distant and far,
Your voice was my guiding star, and I went
towards the voice as slowly it didn't look far,

I was struggling to find my way, but your voice
was the hope guiding through the way,
Suddenly, things changed and the voice that was
so close, started to fade away,
Where shall I go next, I don't know, what to do
next is a new mystery,
With the fog getting denser, my life was getting
tensed,
Miss you my favorite best friend, I am waiting
for you to just rescue me.

When I was Born

It is so simple to celebrate my birth each year,
But difficult to know when I was born,
Was it the day that I opened my eyes and cried for the first time,
When the little me made people around so happy,
Was it my first steps, when I ran through the mud and dirt,
Was it when I walked with a heavy school bag,
Was it when I set out looking for a direction in life,
Was it the moment I made my first strong decision or the simple mistakes that I had made,
I was born on so many days, just like how I was born today
Happy Birthday, Happy Birthday and Happy Birthday.

Memory

I don't remember if I have used this title ever, as there are so many holes that I forget,
Memory is just a lost space with stars revolving around planets,
What should I write is also a question mark, memories that excite or make me laugh,
Should it be those memories that have pain sitting within each bubble called a memory pod,
Another thought is to write about those who were in sweet association with a beautiful loved one,
Then comes a thought: can I leave the burning pores on this and heart?
What to do with these memory holes or memory pods,
Sometimes to forget, you need to remember what the memory says to you,
That is where memories just always stay around like a big clog.

Choices

I've been walking for a long time, just didn't
know to which end,
The road kept on going without sharing the
details of my destinations at all,
The path slowly has a fog coming its way,
making it blurry and unclear to walk,
Still, the mystical fog didn't stop me as it was
my choice to continue the walk,
I wanted to see my destination in the end
thinking it would be beautiful at last,
Suddenly I came to a junction and didn't know
where to go, was it North to the city of beauty or
South to the graveyard of ruins?
While the beautiful flowers blossomed from the
North, the confusion was what if it was flowers
kept in the graveyard in the South,
While long slowly decaying trees showing in the
South, what if those were just branches coming
from the North,

Finally, I decided and started to walk again once,
My decision was to walk towards the south,
maybe the beautiful flowers of the north would have been a great site to watch,
But the choice for South came to mind, to see how life had moved in a full circle
From start to end, I moved to the graveyard and saw what it meant to see life overall.

Void

I always feel a profound emptiness, like a void
that can never last,
I am just a human with simple emotions filled in
my heart, that can just be lost,
Feelings that are hurtful, choices that can be
hurting but still must be made,
I feel that I have a void in my heart that is open,
and I am struggling to close it off,
I am too attached but trying to be free, but these
choices always impact me a lot,
I am also a human who bleeds when gets hurt
and who also has a heart that feels unwanted
going through the harsh words,
This void that is pulling me apart is ripping my
soul which I can't keep intact,

I just know that my void has a cure, but will I
get that cure for sure?
It's love and affection with no questions asked,
It's caring and supporting selfishly in the manner
I am looking for,
Can you help close this void; can you be mine
with no conditions at all?

Skyfall

It's pink with flames red and hot,
It's not how it should be but seems like a war going around,
It's explosion and heartaches which just keep the sky lit up,
It's loss and grief that just aggravate the situation a lot,
I look up and see ashes which are so different but still look like snowflakes,
Feels the sky will fall but it is holding itself a lot,
I am confused to see the strength but still feel scared a lot,
As if the sky is whispering in my ears and telling me that,
Paint me again blue, white, and black,
These colors, red and pink, make me feel that I am falling fast a lot,
If I say,
If I may say,
If I can say it looks like it's a SKYFALL.

Melody

The search is on but still, I am lost, not sure where we are,
Music hits a separate note, but the guitar still says no great song,
I am thinking what to do with the piano that is staring at me from afar,
It is giving me various looks telling me it has been ages since I touched it last,
Melody is what is missing, and I see it getting detached further apart,
I see no help, so I think to get some help from the nature that surrounds me so far,
Chirping birds have beautiful voices but still the fun and joy seem missing,
When I come back with no result that day, the instruments look at me again and frown upon,
I tell them that melody is missing, I am in search of that, be it nature or in my heart,

Dealing with so many words that just bring stress, my mind seems to be in a complete mess and falling apart,
This melody will also help me destress and think clearly a lot,
Melody is still missing, don't know the reason why,
Feel as if it has abandoned my music and thoughts,
The guitar looked at me with some sympathy and said, “Pick me and let me help play some chords,”
Piano said, “Don't worry if you play the wrong keys, maybe that will make a new song,”
With this new faith, I started my journey again, hoping to discover the melody back on this path.

Open Eyes

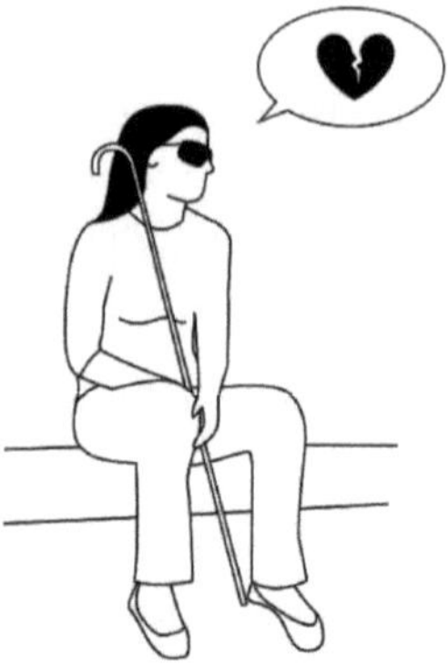

My eyes may be open, but I am still asleep,
With pain and sorrow comes a lot of grief,
The darkness around me confines and limits,
making it hard to take steps forward,
With my limited vision, I see little, and the
beauty around still feels so blocked,
I want to see the color splashes, but they run
away from me,
My eyes may seem open, but does this vision
show anything to me?
The light is lost in these eyes, it makes no
picture as I am what they call *blind,*
My eyes may be open but I am still in a deep
sleep,
Blindness is a gift I received but it haunts me
and causes so much grief,
My eyes are open, whether I am awake or
asleep.

Alone

The path that stands ahead of me is lonely,
As I walk on it, I talk to myself so that I don't
feel lonely,
People who see me crossing different cities
while talking to myself will wonder if I'm
strange,
Although they make no attempt to connect with
me, so I am lonely,
I don't halt or stop, I just keep walking by myself
as my self-talking guide reminds me that I am
lonely,
This choice of being alone can be hard but my
heart has closed itself in so many ways that now
it is lonely,
Burning emotions have consumed everything
around, making me lonely,
Ashes can just be found in those closed doors of
the heart, after which I become lonely,

Need a resurrection with some faith and warm love, so that I can leave behind this tag of being lonely,
Need just care and support as I have cried so many times in loneliness,
Till I find that support and love back again, I am alone in this path of loneliness.

Frozen

I see, I am stuck in the pool of ideas and thoughts,
I have no place to go, neither to the left nor to the right,
They were warm for some time, but slowly got cold,
As if they are dying and it is making me feel scared a lot,
Slowly it's the coldness and the smoke which surround me as a fog,
I am frozen in a field of my own mind's thoughts,
I feel the warmth fading away, what to do is not so clear,
Shall I ignite a flame and risk burning all my memories and thoughts,
Is this the place where I need to stay, a winter bliss that surrounds me, so to say?

Can this heart feel some warmth again,
It is getting colder as I write, with hand
trembling a lot,
Then I hear a voice that is so beautiful that I
wish it had come sooner and saved me like now,
It's the voice of a young boy asking to play with
him, which is a simple task,
I see the cracks in the frozen pool, I am free at
last,
Thank you, my dear son, your simple request
opened the door of my mind a lot,
I saw myself stuck, I saw myself struggling and
now I see myself free from the frozen pool of
thoughts.

Words

I slept and felt as if I will never wake up,
Eyes were looking for a bright light which never appeared,
Suddenly, I see a thunder strike and saw a field surrounding my sight,
Didn't know where I was but still could just see so many scattered alphabets,
Covered in blood—was that my blood that had oozed out? I had no injury, so it was hard to tell,
I picked up a few alphabets and put them together, trying to see what can be made,
Due to that, my hands were covered with blood but silly me I thought it was not present then why suddenly it has come,
The word I could make was "Life," but it slowly caught fire by itself and turned to ashes,

Again, I started to try to create a word that would stay and be present,
It was difficult as the alphabet now just hopped off, with no information that they could do this I had perhaps,
After gathering some of them, I made the word "Happiness," but that was also a short-lived one,
It slowly just faded away, I opened my eyes to find that it was a dream, still confused, I had my coffee with cream.

Wings

I am not sure why, but I have these wings,
I am no God but a simple human being yet still,
I have these,
I am no saint but a person who indulges in
emotions like jealousy, anger, rage and other
worldly activities, so why these wings?
I am just thinking about what these wings are
for, I have no quality that makes me worthy of
these wings,
I move around with these wings, which are
strangely looked upon by people wondering why
I'm not enjoying the flight,
"Walking around like us but he has such
beautiful wings to move all around,"
I get in the elevator and take all the space,
causing people to frown upon me, questioning
why I can't just fly and make space for normal
people in the elevator,

People on the sidewalk are jealous as they feel
they have no cover due to the cold winter,
"This man is blessed to have these wings, a
natural cover for any season, be it a blizzard or a
rainy shower troubling,"
Instead, I just feel so uncomfortable, not part of
the society where my harmony lies,
Some want them as they see the benefits, some
are jealous as they admit why they were not
selected, and some are angry because I have a
benefit,
I am just stressed with no answers, wanting them
gone, so that I will know where I belong,
A simple hardworking human being; nothing
else suits me.

Dreamers

Looking into the eyes or in between moving them around, conversations are done but nobody is around me,
I speak to myself, trying to find comfort, in the life that has me just waiting around, if someone could voice as well,
The phone buzzes, but it's not a message from a friend to catch up over drinks or for fun,
It's the bank offering a loan and claiming that I could own a bigger house than this one,
You try to light a matchstick in the surrounding darkness, with the hope that it will show the path to a bigger one,
Still with all these thoughts and situations
Beauty may revolve around us and we see the visual in the mind to just dream and feel different,

Mind is a strict teacher and heart is a child with
a sad feeling, but they both still somehow get
along as we are just DREAMERS thinking about
how to survive one more round,
A hope that is so little around that,
I get maybe one day all these beautiful feelings,
people and friends around me come back again,
As we are just DREAMERS thinking about how
to survive one more round,
Just for the audience to know that it is not easy
for a DREAMER to be how it sounds,
It's not looking at dreams with open eyes but just
overthinking it every day,
We are humans with emotions running high, as
we are just DREAMERS thinking about how to
survive one more round.

Coffee and Me

It is strange but it is a great love story,
With a love triangle but no jealousy,
It's water at the right boiling temperature with a brown powder that smells so nice that it can last for hours,
Then the final individual is me, how can you have this love triangle without thinking of me?
This eternal love is Coffee and Me, with water not making a guest appearance but staying as if building a bond between,
Pouring each cup, one by one is a joy to see, it's like Mozart's symphony,
The aroma may be hard for a few as there is no milk or sugar to further complement around,
The sip that you take further intoxicates and makes you love it more, again there is no jealousy in this eternal love,

The coffee powder sliding and mixing with the water is beauty that beholds a different feeling,
With each sip you feel different valleys in your dreams, just moving along,
The various stress and sleepiness just melt away, this love you don't have to be scared of, as it will not betray,
That is my lifelong hope, that it stays around with me as it has stayed for so long.

I am blocked

It is not the social media because of which I am scared,
It is your heart which has no space, for my words or thoughts,
It's not the opinions of other people, the ones that I go out with,
It's the constant wondering if you are thinking of me or not,
I feel I am blocked,
Because it's the heart, soul and mind from where I am lost,
It's not the movies that I watch that excite me,
But the moments spent quietly with you that I miss a lot,
It's not the old memories that run around me,
But the thought of never talking to you again that sucks,

Unblock me from every place please because it is choking me a lot,
And if I leave this world someday without having to speak or see you again,
Please do remember that I am not a bad person by heart and loved you with every breath I had,
Keep me locked in your memories, just in a beautiful box which is nicely sealed.

Dark Chocolate

It's fine and Dark, albeit it's sour, but still feels so nice, it touches each sense of heart,
It's like life which has ups and downs, with dry fruits like beautiful stops,
Dark Chocolate melts in my mouth as butter on a hot pan,
It may taste sour to many but so does life, can you ask any question about that?
Its packaging has the percentage of cocoa mentioned in it and the highest amount is my ask,
I feel like eating raw beans but still it's a heightened sensation, that is what I can say if you ask,
You know it is good for the heart, see the poem has health advice for you to look for,

The question is can the heart stay at one place, it leaps like frogs, moving to different directions and wandering off,
Dark chocolate, you are my love as pure as a golden heart,
Your 90% dark element in the chocolate is so tempting I can never resist that, I say from the bottom of my heart.

Someday when I sleep forever quietly

Someday when I sleep forever quietly,
Remember me as a person who behaved nicely,
Someone who took the arrows and suffered,
Which was known as empathy,
Someday when I sleep forever quietly,
Remember me as a father who behaved strictly,
but his child was the best thing that happened,
Someday when I sleep forever quietly,
Remember me as a person who always said, "I understand"
but cried every night quietly, wanting someone to understand him,
Someday when I sleep forever quietly,
Remember me as a person who laughed, when his heart was still heavy,
Who had dreams of us together but still tried to move on when left alone,

Just remember me as a person who could be just
like you yet still be a bit different,
Crazy but supportive, will fight for you daily,
I think soon it will be time for me to sleep
forever quietly.

My Thread Journey

I thought a lot and decided to start a thread,
What to write and what not to was confusion unsaid,
I thought about sadness as that is present so much these days,
then stopped to think how people will feel if I am so negative,
I thought to write about love as people would love, a love story,
then stopped, thinking I will have to give it a good end, which is a bit far from the true story,
Eventually, I gave up the thought of beginning my thread journey, now without writing and sharing, I feel so distressed.
I feel like I have defeated myself by caring so much about what other people might say,

Also, what content I might have if I lost the
artist that wants to express?
It is time for me to return to the drawing board,
reconnect myself with what I have lost,
The beauty is in the journey they say, I have
started mine, unsure when it will end,
But soon, I will have my Thread, readers reading
and criticizing me for what I said,
The artist might connect with them to improve
to his best, but I will sit next to the few who
appreciated me and said, “Well done for the
fresh start again.”

Open the gates

Open the gates, to the thoughts in your mind
Open the gates, to the feelings in your heart,
Open the gates, to the closed lips and talk,
Open the gates, to have my love reach across,
Open the gates, to the door on which I knock,
As I am just in love with the thought of sitting down and talk,
The beauty in the sound of listening to you is eternal,
My mind has so much pain but the words that you speak are like band-aids which heal me,
Open the gates, for the healing moments I want,
Open the gates, for the rainbows to shower,
Open the gates, for the sun and rain to be together,
Open the gates, for the memories to be unlocked,
Open the gates, for you and me to be together once again,

Call me again to talk and break the boundaries,
set by the world,
Just make this life less complicated and open all
those doors that you and I both have locked.

I am not over you

Life had brought us together, to fall in love,
It was destiny that made our eyes meet, so we measure the depth of each other,
It was just directions which made us talk, as I explained the way to your destination,
It was the walk that made us companions on the road, if I may add,
Just the journey made me feel bonded with you so close,
Maybe you reached your destination with your loved one, but I am waiting still with hope,
I would pass away probably with this hope, but what beauty would that be?
My eyes may seem closed but they are always watching you,
I will always sense your perfume, be it from a distance or miles,
Those memories are a treasure we both share with each other my love, if I can even call you that,
You may be over me, but I will never be over you in any universe or life.

Wrong but still Happy.

I thought my words had no one hearing them but
I was wrong,
I thought my posts were not associated with
anyone, but I was wrong,
I thought the pain of heartache that I felt was
missing from other people's lives, but I was
wrong,
I thought I was the only one feeling misery, but I
was wrong,
I thought I didn't have many choices, but I was
wrong,
Sometimes I am happy when I am wrong, not
because other people are unhappy,
But because there are so many people to give
strength to be strong,
Someday I will have the strength to stand next to
you and make you feel right,

To the people around me — I hope I can make things right in your life,
My shoulder can be the support you need, I hope I am not wrong,
My hug can help burn your pain away, I hope I am not wrong,
There is so much where right and wrong are often discussed, but I think I am happy to be wrong sometimes so that my connection with you can go on.

You Killed My Heart

My heart had little space, as it was occupied
with tension and craziness,
You were like a fresh ray of sunlight that just
kept me amazed,
Your voice from a distance was something of a
melody that I can't forget,
I was always spellbound, before you decided to
leave the room empty,
My heart's clutter was removed so you breathe
in it fresh,
Now that you are not present there's just wounds
and scars left,
That's how my heart stopped beating and died a
slow death,
I can never blame you as that will trouble my
heart even more,
I can never curse you as that will open old
wounds and scars which my heart can't bear
anymore,

I will wish my life to live in quiet humbleness
but to love someone again will be difficult,
As the memories of you just live around me as
always, now that the room remains empty
forever,
That's how my heart stopped beating and died a
slow death.

Crying

The eyes didn't want them to leave, the mind was talking and telling otherwise,
The heart kept saying you need to do this, the mind was talking and telling otherwise,
The mind was making both realize that they are important and priceless should not be wasted otherwise,
But still slowly, what looked like water were drops of tears, making the world see me cry otherwise,
It will make me feel light, is what the eyes said as the burden and pain that I saw is unbearable,
The heart said let it be shed, so that it can be cleansed, and the world can feel clear,
The memories will be disappearing, and I will never be bothered again and the heaviness that I carry will also go away,
The mind said first to the eyes that you will be free from just holding them but spending them

on someone who doesn't care and is so worthless,
I saw what you saw, and the person needs no part of this, you suffered daily, and life was torn apart,
Then mind said to the heart,"You are scared to face the reality that the person was never truly yours,
You are scared and palpating with fear, hoping the person comes back once again,"
"The person is not worthy and never will remember both of you," is what I say,
Both eyes and heart said, "It's true what you say but we cared so much, giving up was a difficult thing we must say,
Maybe by crying, some part will be better, it will allow us to feel whatever one says to move on,
So, we cry now with all the love we had. Maybe someday it will be that someone will make these a joyous one.

A letter to the old me

I wrote a letter, so that someday I can post it to my address,
If possible, can this go back in time? So that the old me can read this with the instructions posted on the backside,
To go watch yourself and read it aloud, also make no faces as it may sound strange,
The upcoming year will not be the one you want, it holds love, favor, disrespect, and pain,
You will be appreciated and called a favorite, but you will lose the meaning of the word by the end,
Still, it will be okay for you to just carry on, as your soul will say no worries, happy to help everyone,
After this you will be questioned for the integrity that you have, the respect that you lived for and for the faith you showed to many new people starting their term,

Still, it will be okay for you to just carry on as your soul will say no worries, happy to help everyone,
Move ahead for the people you mentored and cared, for the family and their health will jump on the hurt wagon and slice you with a silver dagger,
Still, it will be okay for you to just carry on as your soul will say no worries, happy to help everyone,
Then you will hit yourself, with depression your body will struggle, illness will come closer and bounce on you, show you the true colors it hid so long,
Still, it will be okay for you to just carry on as your soul will say no worries, happy to help everyone,
In between, a writer will rise, try to help you but not sure how much he will survive, your social media presence will increase but if you think you will be famous that is none,
Still, it will be okay for you to just carry on as your soul will say no worries, happy to help everyone,
This letter is not to correct what will happen but just to share what I couldn't with anyone, as the future will still be the same as you always say no worries, happy to help everyone.

You were never mine

I held you so close that you could hear my heartbeat,
I could skip my heartbeat but not the request that you asked,
I was never as close to myself as I was to you,
I was a star, and you were my moon who I always saw and admired,
But when you left, I remembered that you can't hold onto sand that wants to slip away,
I can't hold you against what you want, your desire is not to be with me but to have someone else's heart,
Now I slowly think that "You were never mine,"
I realized it early and not late but had so much hope that I kept quiet and collected within myself,

I thought one day you will agree, truly be mine,
if not, acknowledge this instead that my love did have some special place,
It had some feelings and thoughts revolving around you,
You did feel that jealousy in the same way that I do, it hurt you when I spoke of other women in your place,
It troubled you when I gave them the same shoulder to cry on, as it'd take away your place,
Well, I may be a wolf who would look at the full moon and cry to connect itself,
But instead, I was just a fool who got played and had no place, I feel angry sometimes for how you treated me,
It was my fault to think that a beautiful girl like you was supposed to be with me, still I have no regret, sometimes want to take revenge but there is no place,
Your love has taken it all I know, I am just thinking now about what to do, in that position I keep thinking about our time together,
Maybe "you were never mine" but our time together will live with me forever.

Love isn't enough

Love isn't enough, if you miss the feelings
behind the words,
Love isn't enough, if you miss the strength to
accept me with my flaws,
Love isn't enough, if you may say you love me
but still, I am alone,
Love isn't enough, as the warmth of your soul is
also what I want,
Love isn't enough, as for you it may just be
words, but to me they mean a lot,
Love isn't enough, if you desire money so much,
as if it is bigger than me,
Love isn't enough, as you feel distrusted if you
receive no calls from me,
Love isn't enough, again as I say if you are
going to mention in words,
Love isn't enough, if you feel I am not the best
person for you my love,

Love isn’t enough, if the joy of your smile is lost
in all the fear that you carry,
Love isn’t enough if the feelings of heaviness
can’t be shared with me,
Finally, love isn’t enough, if we are far apart and
can’t feel each other’s pain, in your mind and
heart I may mean the world to you
But love will never be enough if you don’t
express that with simple words, and make us fall
apart.

I'll be with you even at your worst

The tears from your eyes may look to be yours but are mine,
The pain in that heart may look to be yours but is mine,
The depression and anxiety you may feel may look to be your emotions but are mine,
As it's not just happiness but we are always connected eternally,
So, your pain, sorrow and unhappiness at your worst are also mine,
Just like the happiness you always have in other moments those are also mine,
My heart beats in the same manner as yours, the fear that you carry, I live with them too,

I want you to know that you are beautiful in
every way that you ever could be,
You may feel sometimes I don't care for you but
let me tell you that you are always on my mind,
You may be far, but I can sense your smell
around me all the time,
As it's not just happiness but we are always
connected eternally,
So, your pain, sorrow and unhappiness at your
worst are also mine,
Just like the happiness you always have in other
moments those are also mine.

A child that is inside of me.

A child will obey, allow you to grow
but it wants to play and enjoy the waves,
Make sandcastles like no one is watching,
Be beautiful in its own way,
It's careless and free and has so much to say,
Keep that child inside and let it talk in abundance,
As the emotions which it has is not for you to understand,
You can listen and nod your head away, which will make it smile,
It would always be ready with a goal but was unclear because it was to grow and make something of life,
It had a dream but was hidden as it was unclear how to achieve it since it was not in the right place,

Look at it someday and try to make that dream
come true as you are an adult who has the focus
to make that dream stay,
A child will obey, allow you to grow,
Keep that child inside and let it talk in
abundance and play.

A clown that is me

A clown is in me, that just laughs, be it any situation,
A clown is in me, that just keeps a lot of hope,
A clown is in me, that just keeps breaking and building,
A clown is in me, that just burns himself to light the path of others,
A clown is in me, that wants to break the shell yet is limited to a life with close loops,
A clown is in me, that wants revenge and is angry but keeps killing that inside,
A clown is in me, that doesn't want to smile but still does,
A clown is in me, that loves to dance in chaos but instead wants to shout,
A clown is in me, that also feels hurt and wants to cry out loud but does nothing like that,

A clown is in me, that feels like things were just
snatched away from me, and I just watched it go
away with a smile.
A clown in me will soon want to create chaos, so
that people will know that it's not easy to me,
A clown in me soon will want to bring want that
hurt to come back to those people who think
they are the best,
A clown in me is just now laughing, as it is a
stable place for me, although people tell me I am
unstable.

If he wanted to, he could

If he wanted to, he could stay
If I wanted to, I could have stopped him,
If he wanted to, he could express his love more,
If I wanted to, I could have understood him a little more,
If he wanted, he could have fought with me more,
If I wanted, I could understand the care in the fights,
If he wanted, he could have been the soft and comforting human,
If I wanted, I could have cuddled when he was in trouble and feeling down,
If he wanted, he could have spoken about the scars he had hidden all this time,
If I wanted, I could have read the pain in his simple eyes,

If he wanted, he could have tried to fix the relationship after every fight,
If I wanted, I could have tried to keep our relationship as well,
In the end we both lost each other and hugged our new partners: anxiety and depression,
Now we are apart, and talking and fighting is a luxury which we can't afford,
The new partners we have are beautiful and so great that they stay with us always,
We cry with them and that's it, we have no smile around the space we occupy,
We have a lot of open space which is called loneliness and that also is so great that we stay together always.
But sometimes we both think about the so many 'ifs' on top that could have still been a beautiful place for us.

I am yours…

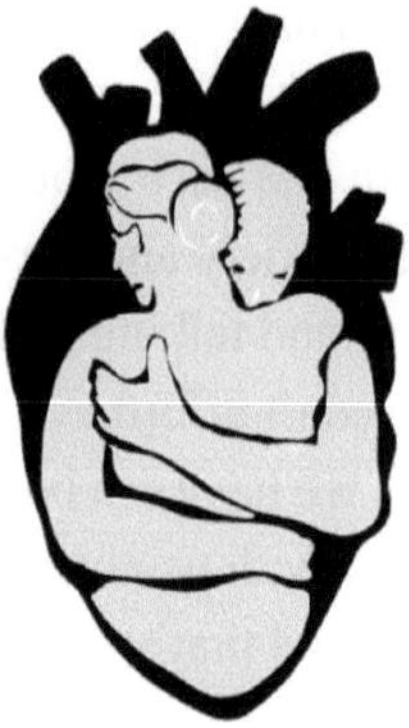

I am yours, was unknown to me,
I was hiding those feelings, that is true, as you were not known to me,
The beauty that you had was not shown to me,
The words you spoke were caring but still unclear to me,
You spoke of love, that is when I found out,
I am yours and you are mine for eternity, that was my thought,
Still, you said it was not like that, you felt something but still denied telling,
Jealousy was so much that you would get angry if anyone else spoke to me,
I am yours, was unknown to me,
Slowly I saw your passion and fell in love with you,

I was bound with restrictions but still cared so much for you,
I was drowning in the sea of love that was shown to me,
I am yours, was unknown to me,
One day when you held somebody else's hand to console, it was hard on me,
Sleeping that night with eyes open was a curse on me,
I just could not feel my heartbeat, I felt it frozen inside me,
I did feel from that day that you were meant for me but by then you had closed the doors,
Told me to stay away always, I think it was the love that told me,
I am yours but need to stay far, that was quickly known to me.

Love at first sight

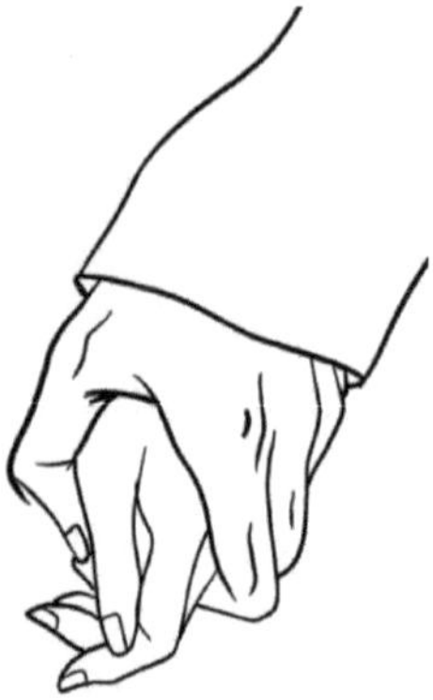

Love at first sight, when those deep eyes entangled me,
It was breathtaking when those words spoke so much to me,
I was thrilled to just spend time with you, with no knowledge of the future,
When I asked the question, what do you think, is there a beautiful life ahead?
As I've been in love with you from the moment we met,
It was a heart-racing feeling to hear what you would say,
I guess I was lucky to know that you said yes,
Everyday post that, was a blessing in disguise, you were my angel,
I knew why, as your heart cared for me always, even when away,

I didn’t need to see you to know when you were happy,
I could tell even with my eyes closed that you thought of me day and night,
That was the eternal connection we shared, that can’t be denied,
This was something that you and I had, it was love at first sight,
Later it was a dream as I woke up when the alarm bell rang to kill my ears,
I didn’t know how to act, I was so close to the most beautiful person and yet still apart,
Got ready and took the bus to the office, sat in a seat, thinking about what had happened to me,
Turned around to a voice, saw you and fell in love again, knowing that it was love at first sight.

You changed

You changed, I don't know why, I am the same,
be it yesterday or today,
I am so lost without you that, I have no place to
be,
The directions are also questioning me and
forcing me to follow,
Where is that shoulder that was once mine
forever,
I am losing my mind, come back and hold me
now,
You have changed, but I am still the same, be it
yesterday or today,
My future is always with you and never away,
Looking from a distance for you now, with no
sight of you, unsure of what to do,
I am at this crosswalk, just waiting and it looks
so weird to me,

People passing by, staring at me with no grace, but with different thoughts,
It feels like a jungle where hyenas are crossing my paths and I am the prey,
You have changed, but I am the still same, be it yesterday or today,
Come look at what is left of me, do you think it was to make me strong,
I am weak and all alone, fighting for the last thing, which are your memories,
You have changed, but I am still the same, be it yesterday or today,
There is not an hour when I can't think about you, you have taught love differently to me,
Comeback and I will never let you go, with so much love filled in me, I will fill it in both our hearts,
Don't change as you are the same, be it yesterday or today, and so am I.

Your Love is Different

So, your love is different now, when did it become different?
Did it become different now that you are 29 and I am 39 years old,
But I thought love always said "Age is no barrier for anyone,"
Is it because I am older and more mature? but I thought you felt secure with that,
As I would always take care of you, help you if you were being immature,
Was it that you feel that I can't pamper you, but I have done that in the past also, have you forgotten so quickly in a day or two?
Has it changed because you feel I will only talk about ideology and give you nothing but advise all the time,
Well, you know we have had a great time laughing at silly things together, talking endlessly with me taking all your tantrums,

Did your love change because we speak
different languages, but I felt till the time I
understood you, it didn't matter,
Love always said it knows no boundaries of age
or language, still your love changed, why, if I
may ask?
I tried to learn your language, tried to be the
same as how you were,
So that you don't feel ashamed in front of your
friends, but maybe my efforts are a bit less,
Did your love change because we belong to
different castes, as you would have had a tough
time adjusting to my house,
I thought love said I am above religion, caste,
language or age, is what I had in my head
wrong?
It would have been tough for me as well to be
around your family with a different caste, maybe
less than what I would have asked,
Still, I would have tried not to change, never felt
out even if it was purposefully made by anyone,
As for me you are my only ask, my love is the
same, though you can be with anyone, I will still
be yours.
Even if I am connected to anyone, I still think of
you and remember our love which lasted a few
days, but I am happy with what you gave.

Time travel of a difference

I wanna go back to the time when you first told me your name,
So that I can make time freeze, the world frozen would be so great,
It will be just me seeing you and feeling the different days,
When we share laughs and enjoy every small break,
An attempt that this spell will never break,
I wanna go back to the time when you first told me your name,
So that I can completely keep that beauty in my eyes,
Shut it down forever and never open it ever, as that is when I sleep forever,
I wanna go back to the time when you first told me your name,

So that I can click a moment and put that down in frame,
Make it a cherished moment, I know I will cry a lot with it but that is fine,
I wanna go back to the time when you first told me your name,
So that I can tell you what happens in our future, how we come close and lose each other,
How things just fall apart, and I never see you talk, you leave me forever with someone else,
After that seeing your smiling face as if I made a big joke, created a strange alternative universe,
I wanna go back to the time when you first told me your name,
So that I can ask the questions I never got answers for, for which I am still struggling,
Fighting every day and making myself suffer with anger again and again,
I wanna go back to the time when you first told me your name,
So that I can thank you for being beautiful, and just the way you have been as it is great, and I don't want a single thing to change.

I hate you.

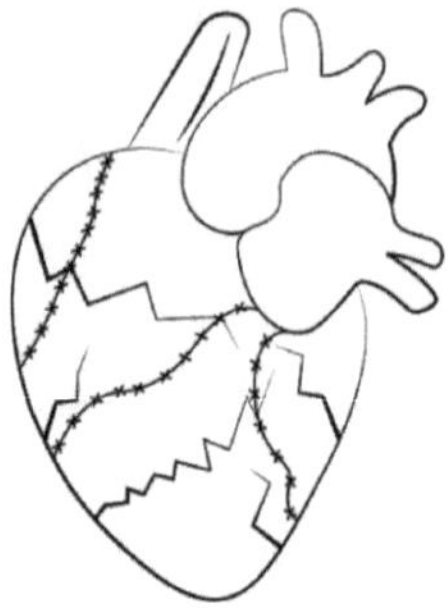

The dry feelings in you are known to me,
I have many thoughts, which are known to me,
I may have been loving and caring, which is unknown to you,
I have some boundaries as well, of feelings, which are known to me,
So, I just say the simple words: let's be unknown to each other,
I can't say I hate you, as I once loved you, which is known to me,
You know the feelings yet are still quiet, you know my despair but are still silent,
The words that you said, I felt the promise seems to be gone now,
Yes, I was hard with words sometimes but so were you with some of your actions, which is known to me,

You can think that I am comparing us now, but
you and I are not so different, see it once and it
will be known to you,
You love me as well but still are distant, which is
something known to me,
You got played by the wisdom of others, which
is known to me,
That is why thinking of hating you, feels
sometimes unknown to me,
For me, loving you always is what is known to
me,
So, again I just say the simple words: let's be
unknown to each other,
I can't say I hate you, as I once loved you,
which is known to me,

Blood Moon

I am a lover that loves the moon,
I am not an admirer but see her in the moon,
I get flowers and sit down on a bench to share my feelings with her,
People say I am mad, but I love the moon,
The day it is the lunar eclipse, I am so sad as I don't see her,
Some place partial and someplace complete, that is my horror,
I am jealous of the stars as they take my space,
Are so close to my love while I am miles apart, still I love the moon,
I am a Wolverine who loves my blood moon always,
She is a trickster, people say, as she keeps you so far and at bay,

Whenever she is close causes such a problem, a
huge tide of waters that just flow through,
Why do you wanna keep loving that red moon
like a wolf? Stay late and howl, making
everyone scared,
I have no answer for them but just to say, that
she was a friend who said she would always
stay,
She fulfilled her promise by coming back to me,
though not in human form, but still in a beautiful
spherical being,
I know it's my love as we are connected, don't
disrespect us by calling us soulmates,
We are friends that just grew together, and this
tale has not ended but will be forever.

Overthinking

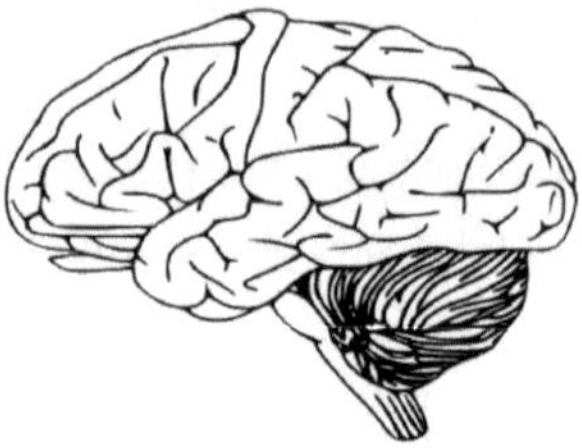

My mind is a constant machine with no kill switch,
I overthink things which you can't imagine yet,
I am always thinking about what to do and how to behave,
What will be liked and what will be hated,
For once, I want to relax with no thoughts ever,
Just sleep in your lap, if it is forever that will be great,
That sleep would be so good, resting with no thoughts or anything,
I still feel that the mind just keeps running like a live wire,
Whether I'd sleep or not is going to be a question unanswered,
As I will still be thinking about you, as after my permanent sleep, what will you do,
How will the pain be for you? Will you be relaxed?

Will you remember me or leave me like a chapter?
Will you move on or will you be stuck on me forever?
As this mind keeps thinking on, I don’t think I will get any help from it ever,
I just hope someday things change and my overthinking rests and my mind is free again.

Love is known or Unknown

My love, though I confessed to you, but still it seems to be unknown to you,
Your feelings are known to me, which I've been appreciating as prominent, known to me,
You still deny your love thinking it is okay for me,
I love you and I try to express but you get angry,
I have tried many times to keep my mind away and feelings inside,
Love is known or unknown to you, is not known to me,
It is so easy for you to behave detached and not associated, it is a surprise to me,
It is difficult for me to lose you every day and I can't mention it as I think you know that,
Seeing you go away with someone else is difficult but still, I stand at the corner,

See and tell my heart that maybe she is still unknown to love,
Sometimes I feel I also don't understand love, as sometimes everyone who cares, can I love them all?
Yes, I can, some as friends, someone with respect, but love to you was special,
Love is known or unknown to you, is not known to me,
Lost to be in love, I think I just aim for attention,
Probably love was never known to me, as it seems so unclear to me.
Love is known or unknown to you, is not known to me.

Real Connection is hard to find

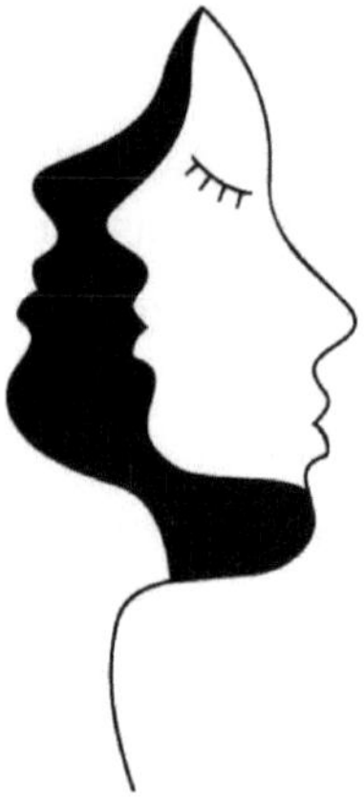

I felt you and I were connected, not since today but since always,
I felt you and I were meant to be together forever,
I felt you were beautiful, and I was handsome, complementing each other,
Little did I know that I was never your expectation,
Your beauty bedazzled me, and my words charmed you,
Little did I know that I was never your expectation,
I felt you and I had something but that was not the case,

That is when I realized Real Connection is hard to find,
I am thinking all the time about what is right and wrong,
I am so emotional I always get lost whenever I hear your voice,
I want to be around you and always surrounded by you,
Little did I know that I was never your expectation,
That is when I realized Real Connection is hard to find,
I always had a path for my life, but after you came along, I wanted us to walk that path together,
Now you are gone, I am pathless, just going all around hopeless,
I am so desperate for love and support I knocked and kicked so many doors,
Trying to find a connection that makes me feel happy and strong,
That is not what is meant for me I guess, living alone is my life's next maze,
Little did I know that I was never your expectation,
That is when I realized Real Connection is hard to find around.

Humanity

It's a topic that is so overrated,
people say many things but their actions tell a different story,
My religion may differ, but I'm still a human,
The pain we experience is the same,
Regardless of our religions, the success is same be it me, or someone with a different religion,
Our practices are different, but body organs are the same,
Then why can't I have a religion of humanity with just a small little space,
I am still confused, before I was born, this was never told to me,
It came with a different language that caused more boundaries,
Yes, they taught us in school to respect each other's religion,
Enjoy all the festivals together, although there were just holidays for me,

Though as I grew up, I realized all those rituals were necessary,
Still, we harbor hatred for each other knowing all these things,
Just a small spark causes unwanted things to get escalated,
I just think if we had Humanity, would it not be good with similarity?
I am just a small person with no knowledge, I hope someone out there can understand.

Eternity of Wishes

I am writing a list, that may seem long,
Don't worry these are small wishes from my heart,
They may seem an eternity long,
Don't worry these are small wishes from my heart,
I am trying to fulfill each as I go along,
Don't worry, these just look long,
I am happy to show you what they are made of,
Be my friend and look in my heart as they will show you what I mean,
Don't worry, these are small wishes from my heart,
I am just a small dot in the big dot of the universe,
That has a heart also which wants some bit of the wishes to come true,
They are beautiful as they present love for each one,

Don't worry, these are small wishes from my heart,
I am writing them on a page, hoping to create a simple phrase,
Praise me if my attempt is beautiful and not wrong,
Don't worry, these are small wishes from my heart,
Quietly in this life if I can fulfill a few, that would be wonderful,
I will have a sense of relief in my mind, that life was fast, but some wishes got fulfilled while some left behind,
Don't worry, these are small wishes from my heart,
It may seem that it's a line I say many times, but it is true that the list is not long,
Hope the small wishes from my journal can be passed through,
I am just hoping if not me, someone else will make the rest true,
Don't worry, these are small wishes from my heart,
Now is the part when I close this poem, hope you read till the end with thoughts of your wishes in mind,
So, to all I would say just these few words, that your wishes are also just small wishes from the heart.

Beauty of my Age

I am going to be 40 in just a few months,
People may consider it old and so do I,
Some say it is still young, don’t think you are old otherwise,
I lost people who wanted to be surrounded by someone better,
An older person with dark hair like me was a shame, despite my maturity and the lessons I offer,
I can still fight like a young person, though my breath may falter in between,
When young people can say, “Old uncle, don't try,”
Still to stay alive, I hit the gym, the machines don't question me why,
Motivation flows through, that's the Beauty of my Age, don't question why,

Beauty of my age is that I am old to be mature
and guided to be the best person at your side,
Give you real love and comfort as I have lived
long enough to know the true meaning of each
one,
Learning the art of silence, as to speak many
words now is not my type,
That's the beauty of my age, now you know,
don't ask me why.

Dancing With Shadows

I see the sun go down, and slowly the night falls,
It's beautiful the way it happens and slowly what the world becomes,
The roads are lit with candles and very minimal light,
It is another magical moment in sight,
What is beautiful can't be described in words,
Let the imagination run a little wild overall, and see what comes up,
I sit near the corner on the staircase of a house,
it's a cold night and I keep a candle nearby,
Windows from behind on every floor has candles lit up with people moving about,
The shadows on the wall, with mine joining them, makes me see another masterpiece,
It seems like moving shadows are dancing to a music piece,

Mine just now asked a lady, if she'd be happy to join,
As it's the last song of the night, if she can be close to my heart and dance,
I know morning will come and the magic will be gone,
I sit every day and see at night how the magical dance gets recreated by the candlelight.

When Death Smiled

I was a simple foot soldier who had no place but in the war,
It was beautiful whenever I picked up my shield and sword,
The day came when the fear came to my mind and heart,
There were just a thousand of us but fighting an army whose numbers were hard to count,
My soul was down as to how to fight this adversary so strong,
Numbers that were not in thousands but lakhs,
I just went to war thinking nothing, but had your thoughts in my heart,
My heart was thinking, "Who will take care of you when I am gone?
Still, I marched with less fear and anxiousness just at heart,

Swords and blades that were rusted but still
used, clashed hard,
Going through the Archers and then the
horsemen was my plan,
I charged into the army that was in the north,
fought everyone in my path,
Just then, a few hits went through my armor and
that is when I smiled,
Blood was oozing through my body, but my
adrenaline was high,
Death smiles at all of us I thought, we mere
thousands having to lose but ourselves,
That is when I saw the Angel of Death staring at
me from a distance, and then disappearing
suddenly,
My end was near I felt, that is when slowly the
Angel of Death approached me with a smile,
I smiled back and said, “It is not today my friend
that I am coming,”
That is when I hit him with a blow of my sword,
smiled back and then slowly turned away,
I feel my war for today is done, someday I will
go smiling again but it could be the final breath,
you never know.

Poetry Of Pain

Yes, everyone would say, this is no different than poetry of pain,
It will be about heartbreak and so on, a boy or a girl suffering with their time in love, will be the thought,
This is still a different poetry frame,
The pain of a hard-working boy trying to rise to fame, working for siblings to be on the right path,
That is his fame and not a celebrity tag that he wants, sells small goods in the market,
Some day bought and some days nothing in hand,
Still takes the disappointment of this pain back, when enters the house smiles and doesn't complain much,
This is how he lives daily but, in his heart, knows that one day he will succeed,

He is a person with passion, a heart filled with action,
He is waiting for his moment in life, fighting all obstacles and never fearing life's tough sides,
He is present in the market area to sell his goods, be it rain or harsh sunlight,
He is ready from his heart and knows that his fame is not far from his sight,
Moving ahead can be a challenge sometimes but hoping to be hopeful is what he has in mind,
I can probably learn a few things from his passion, I may be privileged but hope someday he becomes big, and I see him shining as he should
Till we meet next my buddy, always keep your heart golden and work your way steadily to the top.

Beautiful Heart Of Yours

It is not very difficult to say that you have a pure heart,
Your intentions are as bright as a clear blue sky,
The heart feels touched by the concerns that you have,
I can see in your eyes you are in love with me,
I can't deny that a beautiful heart like yours should always be mine,
I just hope I am always what you are looking out for,
As I am unable to match the feelings that you have, the simplicity that you possess,
I am just a simple person, and you are the best,
I am not sure, what you found in me that was so likable,
You said I was your favorite and that is what I know is beautiful,
You took my pain and suffering away by just listening to me,

When I cried, your shoulder was always present
to tell me that you will always be with me,
I slept in your lap when I couldn't sleep with
anxiety, as if I was a small baby,
I am always scared that this world will conspire
and take you away,
I will be left shattered as so many people are
scared of you and me,
They can never understand what we share is a
true bond, your heart is beautiful just like you
are,
I may be a little crazy and loud, but that is how
we complement each other,
I could write endlessly about you, still I would
say: I can't live without you,
So again, I say the Beautiful Heart of Yours is
just so lovely to have in my life, I am mad about
us, and that's a fact of life.

Love the way you are

I love the way you are, so clear and open from the heart,
You make me feel special all the time, it is so important that you are mine,
I want to take care of you all the time, be it day or night,
The beautiful eyes that you have, have a depth that I have no submarine to dive into,
Your lips are soft and tender and speak words so beautiful that I lose my thoughts,
I am just running in circles trying to find a clear way, though your beauty is difficult to pass,
My lady, my darling, whatever I call you, it is always difficult to grow apart,
You need to be around me, or else I can only be jealous of the people surrounding your path,
You're a celebrity who has so much stardom that I feel lost, I am just a small person in the

audience who feels he is made only for you, my love,
Love the way you are as it's the most beautiful way that I can see anyone in my life so far,
You are with a simple man, somewhat of a Blackstar but I love you just the way you are,
I may not be able to offer you luxury or so many gifts, my dear one,
Still I can provide you with all the love you want,
I can make you angry sometimes, off and on with the words that I say, and the laziness shown so far,
Still, I can cook a nice meal for you and make a candlelight dinner if you want,
What I know for sure is this simple fact: I just love the way you are.

Raging Storm

I feel a sudden pain inside myself, as if
something just broke within me,
I feel a sudden heaviness in myself, as if I am
carrying a lot of weight,
I feel a sudden disbelief in myself, as if I am
trying but reaching nowhere,
I feel a sudden mistrust in myself, as the world is
standing against me,
With all these disappointing feelings, I should be
broken with no pulse within me,
Still, I feel like a fire that is burning within me,
as fumes are flying all over,
I focus and try to push what is left within me, I
am burning like a volcano,
As I carry a Raging storm within me,
From where this storm came within me when I
questioned looking at the mirror,
It broke as it could not face the intensity in my
eyes,

It is like revenge is sitting inside of me, against the people who conspired,
I was cornered and massacred with no escape route left for me,
It is difficult to suggest that life is still left within me,
But I know a raging storm that keeps rising within me,
I look at my sides, but they seem to be burning as usual with nothing left in the path,
I dine in hell is what is my heart currently telling me, the storm is building slowly,
As the smiles drain and quietness falls within me, I want no contact and be isolated
This is the true nature that is building now within me,
As I carry a Raging storm that grows within me,
The only way I see is to vent this out, build myself and take my revenge now,
I am not that strong as of now and it is delaying daily, I don't think I even have the support of the almighty,
Still, I move around quietly, as I carry a Raging storm that grows within me.

Quiet Notifications

The phone used to ring so often with
notifications from you,
I used to write so much even when I was not
used to, for you,
I always wanted to talk, call you and sit down in
front of you,
Spend hours and make sure you talk while I just
listen with no interruptions,
It was very beautiful every moment that we had
like that,
What was cute were the various times when a
misspelled word would create a mini-storm,
It was hurtful at first, but we would always
resolve it later as if nothing had happened a few
minutes back,
It was the golden period of the relationship that
we had, at least I thought we had something,

That was not actually how you felt, and things
changed slowly when you left,
Those notifications were nothing but just
questions now,
The feelings of asking the various questions of
concern and care are gone,
So much has changed, I don't know what to say
or what not to,
Only place now I can see you smiling is when I
close my eyes, as you have gone away so far,
The long talks have become limited to what you
must respond when a question asked,
These quiet notifications are what I am left with
now, I know I am not happy but still who is
asking me that?
I am never asked by anyone, "How are you
doing?" or "Do you have some pain to talk
about?"
I still feel now, I am away, and no one needs me,
as I am not that important for anyone to ask
about,
They say keep your expectations less, but even
after so much respect, I got crushed,
Quiet notifications, Quiet notifications, is all that
my heart knows now, I wonder why I even have
a phone at all.

Even If I am Broken

Some days I question myself when I sit down:
what if life was good?
Some days I question myself when I sit down:
what if relationships were good?
Some days I question myself when I sit down:
what if things were normal?
Some days I question myself when I sit down:
what if I did not have this much free time?
Then one day, someone very close to me asked
me to see if I want to change the question,
Sit down and think, even if you don't have a
good life, still you are alive
Sit down and think, even if relationships have
been cheating you, you found the worth of them,
Sit down and think, even if relationships
abandoned you, did that bring you closer to
yourself?
Sit down and think, even if things are not
normal, still life is going around,

Sit down and think, even if you have free time,
your efforts to be engaged have lost its hope?
My mind still fighting to see how to deal with
things going around,
Are my *what-ifs* superior or the *even-ifs*
supportive? Who knows but I must find,
As the questions are mine to answer, to think
and identify, what my various thoughts are,
Currently, I am broken to the core, the *what-ifs*
and *even-ifs* are mood swings that just come and
go,
Something positive should happen so that my
mind re-ignites and finds the path which I lost,
I broke myself by being angry and not calm, still
it was me and none who took those steps,
Even if I am broken, hope those pieces can be
glued together, for still there's a long way left
for my life,
A beacon of light is all I want, that would just
bring a happy person back to my heart, with all
questions finally answered,
All doubts would finally be gone, even if I am
broken I still have these words to say.

The Red Horizon

The horizon was never known to me, I had never seen the sky meeting so openly,
For me, the sky was always far, someplace where I could see the Sun, Moon and stars,
Science taught me so many things, saying that it is just an imaginary line,
Still, I felt it was something different from other places,
It can't just be an imaginary line but has so much to say,
It must have seen so many phases and so many changes, still is quiet within itself,
Does the horizon have anyone to talk to, or is it lonely as a Blackstar,
Who just stays in a corner and people say things about when they have a poem to mention,
Is it just a word for them to compare aspects, that it has lost its meaning,

Has the horizon become someone who is okay
with how things are or does it want to speak to
nature as others do?
That is when traveling in an airplane, I saw the
horizon outside the window,
Glowing with the redness of the sunset that was
about to occur,
Slowly came to my window and knocked and
said quietly, I know what you are thinking of,
I am just a normal meeting point, allowing the
sun and moon to talk with the stars just jumping
to say what they want,
It's a quiet laughter that keeps me alive filled
with the tales they share,
It's the poets that mention me in their poems,
making me included in someplace,
I may be called an imaginary line but still taught
in a class,
Yes, I would have loved a companion as well,
but that was never the thought,
I still get the colors of Sun coming up and going
down, making me a Red Horizon after all,
Once the Moon comes black, color falls and I
can also close my eyes for some time and relax,
Oh, I forgot to tell the clouds, come and tickle
me sometimes with the lightning bolt that they
have,
Also, air whooshes them away when they
become too naughty for me after all,

That is when the air hostess came and said we are getting ready for landing,
I felt like I was dreaming, but when I saw the red horizon again with a small cloud forming a smiley in the sky,
Telling me that it was no dream, but a beautiful conversation I had with the Red Horizon on a silent Sunday night.

I am a Devil but an Angel too

I am a Devil, banished from the heaven,
Notorious and full of mischief,
The details I could never tell my father, that it was not just me but so many others,
My father and me had a different relationship, something that I think the humans learned from me,
I could never say many things to him although I was an angel, and he couldn't hug me, as he was the King of Heaven,
Although I was banished from heaven to carry out my duties in hell, the devil also needed vacations who will question my will,
"Open your eyes and tell me your desires," was my question when I enjoyed my holidays outside of hell,

Love was which struck me though, people reminded me that I was the devil and have duties to fulfill,
Can I leave this love behind? So I asked her as well, what is that you desire,
She picked someone else, and I stood by and saw the picture with my eyes,
It was her desire to pick someone else, not my love, but to be with someone else,
I know if she ever calls me for help, she'd be my priority, no questions asked,
She did leave me, and I went back to the throne that I had in hell,
Devils also mourn and cry, people need to know that as well, only my bad side is exposed,
The desires fulfilled for so many are unknown, yes that was the guilt they suffered,
I had to make sure those desires are short-lived, and punishment was to be given,
Although everyone reminded me of my duties, that love of mine was never afraid of me,
She openly said to me laughing once "You are my favorite devil, you are my number 1."
Still, you need to remember one thing "Maybe you are the Devil, but Angel too, my darling,"
I am banished from heaven, and she can never come to hell, my love story is incomplete, that is why I am the devil.

India's Medal Will Come

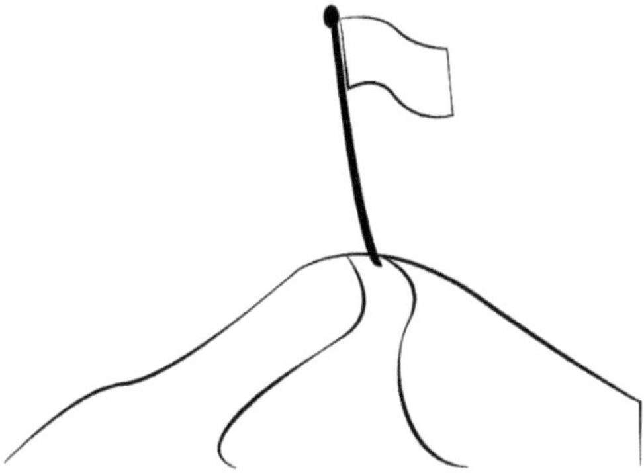

India's medal will come, we will win with the efforts done,
Prepare ourselves with all the things needed,
Show the sportsmanship not just on the field but also off the field,
One nation united we go ahead and make sure our efforts never fail,

You can ask me the questions, we did win medals Bronze and Silver,
Yes, I am proud of that but it's time to eye the gold one,
Not just in one game, shooting or wrestling but in many others as well,
See how the top countries performed, learn our lessons and prepare ourselves well,

This dream to get gold medals in all games
should not be let down,
Let's start preparing ourselves now itself, for the
future will be ours too known,
India's Medal will surely come, let's treat our
athletes also as a team to form,
Let's focus on Badminton, Javelin Throw,
Hockey, and Boxing, to just name a few,

Let's have the right facilities for all the games
including cricket as well,
Let's rush to the stadiums, not just when these
games are in India but outside as well,
India's Medal will come, it is an igniting feeling
knowing we are united as one,
Let's start tournaments for all such sports, like
we have for cricket so many times,

Let's be equally disappointed and encouraging
when we have a loss,
Let's make an effort to teach these sports to our
younger ones,
I know for a fact that this can be done, India's
Medal will come.

7 Days and 7 lives'

A week has 7 days, and I have 7 floors where I live,
It's just a small journal of 7 days, looking at 7 different lives
I am the writer, so mine comes first to begin with, also as I live on the ground floor,
I am the best-known to all the others in the building so far,
I am simple but still complex, sometimes romantic, sometimes angry, it's a mix,
I am just 39 years old, but want to keep myself not more than 25, confusing after all,
Next comes the sweet couple on the first floor, I gave my introduction on Sunday so 1 day had gone,
The couple leaves the door of the lift unlocked as they have a beautiful loud discussion,
Well, Monday, being a working day for a few, the couple also had their office and discussions,

As we move forward in the week, we have Tuesday with the second floor, a nice religious family lives in it,
They don't eat chicken and frown upon me whenever I cook it, as the lovely little son enjoys that a lot,
Comes to me just to have it after all,
Are you good at math and keeping some count, we have had 3 days, and 3 lives talked about
As the title of the poem says 7 Days and 7 Lives'
I hope you didn't think it was my different life 'coz that would be crazy, I can't handle that many relations,
4th day is a beautiful Wednesday, and the 4th floor is also beautiful as a couple recently wed came to stay,
They are nice people to everyone, they are simple as they are from out of town, so very new to this place, slowly making friends,
Husband is a workaholic as he comes home late, wife understands and goes to meet the parent-like-couple who stay on the 5th floor,
Oh my god, see the day changed! It quickly became Thursday, the old couple are the most respected in the building and they help whenever needed by anyone,
Moving on to Friday, see the weekend coming in a big way, so we climb the ladder for the 6th

floor, that place is locked and the owner is out of
town,
He is a businessman with a wife and two kids,
that's all I know, also they are looking for
tenants,
Do you know if anyone is looking for a space?
We are arriving on the 7th floor, and we have a
crazy script writer or you can say poet,
He is not a big shot but pretends to be one,
see, it is Saturday and a week is already gone,
He has glasses and a beard, maybe he just wants
to be a conventional writer always,
I hope you did the math while reading this on,
we had 7 days and 7 lives to look out for,
See, I forgot to tell you that this building is
located in Hyderabad, just near the airport
highway.

Ghostwriter

It was a very hard day filled with work,
As I had a deliverable due the next day, focusing on detail was my mind,
I thought of each detail, what needed to be provided,
The office was lit up when I had walked in,
Slowly the lights began to fade as people started to leave,
I was not so tense since it was not the first time,
I just kept working, even when my friends at 2:30 PM in the afternoon left,
The shift they were working was done, they had come so early,
Now they were just thinking of reaching home and dozing off,
Coffee was badly needed for me and my friends who walked in at 2:30 PM,
They will be present till midnight, that was crazy timeframe for them to work,

How do they do it, I always thought but still at least they got time to wake up late,
I needed to concentrate on work again and focus, that was not lost,
I ended up staying post-midnight, with just a light shining on top of me,
I still have work to focus on, but needed a cup of coffee as my mind was jammed,
I came back to my seat and saw the screen was on, and a notepad open,
And it was written, "You are not alone, my friend."
First, I thought it was a prank but then realized there was no one,
I closed the notepad and sat down to continue work when the pad opened again, and the keyboard just started typing by itself,
It was so scary and chilling to the core that I fell from my chair, and looked up to see a figure just like me in a spirited form,
It said, "It's good to work so hard but it's even better to ask for help when you know things will be tough."
Further it said, "Look at yourself—all messed up. Live a little," and then vanished away,
That's when I realized: I was the Ghostwriter writing to myself. Life is short, so let's live it a little bit more.

Strange Conversation

Strange conversations always happen, we meet strangers from all walks of life,
Something like this happened with me also once,
When I had a flight that was flying late and I had a lot of time,
I went to the Airport lounge to close my eyes for a while when softly she said,
Can you move to the other side, as I need the charging point,
When I looked at her, she was a nice lady dressed in pink and white,
Since my phone was not charging, I moved to the next seat by her side,
I was about to close my eyes again when I saw a big scar on the left side,
Her face as if had some damage in the past and was operated,

I apologized and then asked, was this due to an accident you had in the past,
She said don't feel sorry, and was okay to answer, she didn't feel bad,
Like the scar was not something to be ashamed of, this confidence was great to see,
We started talking and found that the scar was something to be,
A relationship so toxic went wrong, now she is better and very strong,
Soon her flight announcement happened, she was about to leave,
When she mentioned it was nice talking to you, very carefree,
This little time that we spoke about many things could be considered a general talk,
But the confidence she had even with that big scar was adding to her beauty overall,
Sometimes these are memories and moments we remember,
They might seem small but are very important, beauty lies in the eyes of the person,
She saw that scar was also a beautiful ornament and wore it like a star.

I was the right person

When I distributed the chocolate on my birthday in the class,
When people were sharing various badges especially made for each other,
When friendship's meaning changed in a year from 5th class,
I made a badge for myself at home and smiled looking in the mirror
I know I was the right person, I was the right person,
When everyone in college had a love life, I just kept looking all the time,
When people called me fat because I had a medicine which was needed,
When they compared it with my mental health, and called me a crazy person,

I know I was the right person, I was the right person,
When I started working in office, and was working hard,
Available to learn and share my knowledge with other people around,
When I spend 16 hours struggling, still not having the big paycheck,
Waited for my right moment for more than 16 years, in my heart,
I know I was the right person, I was the right person,
When I had put blood, sweat and heart, never thought of my weakness,
Never focused on who said what but taught people with all the knowledge that I have,
When I thought I could be of some use with the information I give them,
When was conspired behind my back, instigated to get agitated and shout,
Accused of something which I never did, focused still to help benefit others,
Blocked for never ever saying anything wrong,
Unfollowed because I was not the best friend,
Tried to be a leader who was unconventional and fell from the heart for people,
I know I was the right person, I was the right person,

With all said, I continue, sometimes emotionally
hurt and bruised, still have a reason to go to
teach my son how to be strong and that,
I was, I will and always try to be focused to be
the right person.

Where have I reached

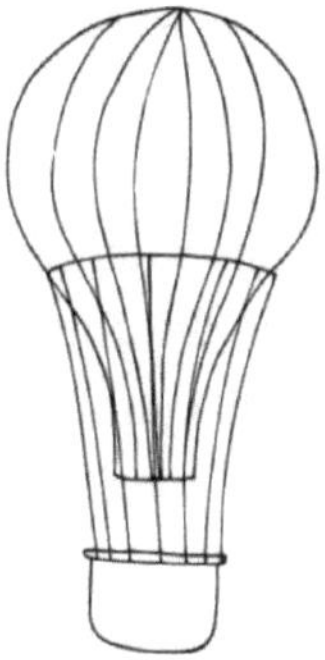

I think I have reached a strange place,
Although it looks to be a country but it's difficult to say,
I saw many things around that looked the same as my hometown,
Still, I feel I have reached a strange place,
A place where a mob runs around, that just want to do what it wants,
A place where our children are lost, they just do whatever they want,
Girls are taught to understand, also be modern and enjoy life,
Misinterpreted they indulge in drinking and strange fights, accusing and put wrong blames,
They are taught right and wrong but still forget as they grow, I see this place full of social media as a teacher, where did other teachers go?

Boys are taught also incorrectly, to take what they want,
If not given straight forward then fight and still take over the need,
They are also taught right and wrong but being forgetful is such a nice thing, they do that as if it is easy to say sorry in the end,
I think I have reached a strange place,
Where I have started shouting and crying in the middle of the road,
Saw people making videos, so that they can easily post on Instagram,
Slowly a person walked up to me, gave some water and talked to me,
That is when he told me about so many things, I realized the world has changed and become this crazy place,
He said he was a poet and spoke about what he was trying to do,
Work with a group and making poetry strong as it used to be,
He still said, to make a difference we need all this support of technology, fight it once
And then see what the new world holds for the new generation,
Either they will see the difference and beauty, or we will lose this battle but with dignity of course.

A Computer that talks to me

It is so strange and difficult to understand that I am confused,
A computer that talks to me and speaks not so humanly,
It still has a computer voice, and it still behaves differently,
Like I can interrupt him by pressing a button and it will not be angry,
I can open a different topic for discussion, and it will reply quickly,
I will ask it to create a picture of me and it will draw,
I can easily ask it the meaning of any word, and it still will have that presented correctly,
This is a not just with my computer only, and I hold no rights for its exclusivity,

It continues to do this task as mentioned by me
and still no food, water or need of a salary,
All it asks is for electricity, that too, if it is a
laptop, it has a battery,
All that I ask him are called prompts that make
him know the task details like an office
secretary,
I am too old to understand this but still trying to
feel it anyhow,
It has been given a fancy name called Artificial
Intelligence, and has so many products like
ChatGPT and many other to be,
Every industry wants it, and humans are scared
of their replacement instantly,
I am a retired person, who just feels like writing
small little poetry,
Sometimes it can easily do that for me, but I feel
it loses my emotion and creativity,
It is adapting and soon probably will replace me
also but that will be end of my time for sure, I
know that fact,
Till that time, I am amazed like a small kid with
a computer that talks to me.

I am a difficult person

I am a difficult person, a person who has the wrong values,
A person who feels that people should be treated right, a person who was in a wrong school after all,
A school where you were taught to respect all and make sure discipline was followed,
I was born probably in a wrong family where I saw hard-working parents and a sibling who loved and cared for me,
Still my incorrect attitude was not tolerated and was correct to tell me the right method,
Hardship which taught me a lot, to dream of a life with no boundaries,
The biggest mistake of mine is being respectful to everyone,

Hoping that they will do the same to me, but it is a way for them to judge me that I am just a "yes man,"
A simple person but still very difficult because I feel, I should help all to walk together,
I still have an alter ego in me, that is surprised by the nice person,
The one who always gives the nice person the benefit of the doubt,
Sometimes it is let out when I shout and get angry that is like firing a cannonball,
And then all the nice things I did disappear, and I am the wrong person for everyone,
Slowly my old alter ego comes back, giving my angry self some water, and allowing some time to cool down,
But by now I have lost all, and I am the bad person, apologies have no meaning,
Still was I not human either, was I not supposed to feel hurt when people left,
When I was smiling still in pain, was I not supposed to have that friend ask me how I was,
Did I have no right to be upset when someone said something wrong to me,
Can I not express grief to the person whom I asked for support,
But yes, I am a difficult person, a difficult person as I am friendly, will try to support you,

try to be friends with you even if I am older than
you,
I am a difficult person, so I must be okay with
staying alone,
Well, I have me, and I have me, but I can
understand you must be busy.

When you came back to me

We meet and just hit it off,
It was different but not love,
You fell a lot for me, and I was a bit surprised,
As no one had ever felt so much for me, they spoke when I initiated the conversation,
But you made some of my scars also heal, as I just needed some words,
I just needed to hear those words and get someone to care,
It felt magical and it felt love, but it was not the same,
I felt each time of love and beauty in every glimpse of you,
You felt I was good, sometimes moody but never thought of anything else apart,
The reality was also fine, the choices we had were ours to find,

One day like all stories, things changed, Feelings
slowly just faded away,
I hated how it ended, At least I could have a
friendship to stay connected,
Still, it was fine, I don't know it was tough for
my mind to move in the right direction,
I felt what if things could be different, slowly I
started changing,
When suddenly one day my notification buzzed,
although I had no hope, but it was yours,
I didn't know how to react, you mentioned you
were standing downstairs,
I rushed to the balcony to find you with your
suitcase and messy hair,
I came downstairs, to meet you but felt that you
had gone through a lot in your life,
Got you upstairs and gave you some water, you
sobbed badly as everyone had given up on you,
I was the last hope and not the first choice, but
that was not on my mind,
Asked you to take some rest as you had gone
through a journey, both travel and in mind,
Later checked how I could help, got you all
settled slowly, and then left,
Checked on you every now and then, that is
when you asked, "Why did you help" and "Why
not shut the door like others"

I replied and said, “It was so tough to think about moving on that I never did,”
But now to think about it again is even more tough, which I had not thought of,
You lost me but still to see you hurt, is a problem,
You have come back with a hope that I can’t break, and that is my choice like how I did in the past myself,
When you came back to me it was amazing, at least you considered me a choice that is a relief, what else to say?

Silent Conversations

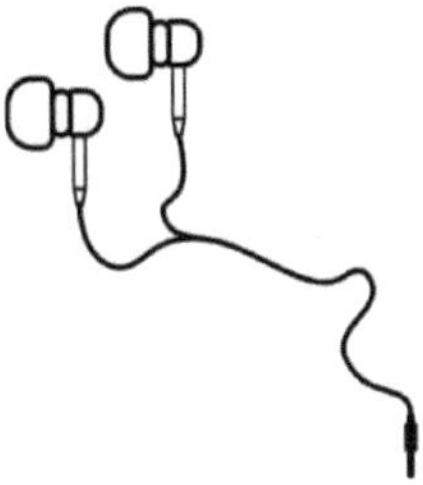

I sat by the seashore, hoping to see the sunset in a quiet view,
To my disappointment, I was not the only one with the same thought,
Many people came and so to cater to them, we had many vendors,
People selling stuff to eat, balloons for kids and other things with their voices so loud,
To add to this, I met a friend, who came and sat with me, talking constantly,
With a view of every point happening in this world, I thought to myself, "Goodbye, my dear sunset,"
I felt if everything froze now, I will not miss my beautiful sunset but that would not be possible,
On the other hand, I had my friend who was talking nonstop, and all these sounds,
In between I wanted to shout, I had a vision where I am shouting at all,
They become quiet, and I enjoy the sunset after all,

Well, all of this were hopes and dreams, a silent conversation between me and myself,
That is when I closed my eyes and for a few minutes, stayed like that, post that opened my eyes,
Saw myself transported in a different reality, where all the noise was gone, it was just my friend going on,
That is when I asked if we could sit quietly for a few minutes and I found no disagreement in that,
Then I was watching my beautiful sunset after all, when the red-hot ball, said a few words to me,
I looked to the side to see who it was as I could not believe the sun could talk,
Silently whispered a few words to me and they traveled the ocean to come to me,
That is when I heard the words come together and say,
"Don't worry about the noises around you, just enjoy the beauty that is around you,
See where I end, and that will bring some great vision to your eyes"
Slowly all noises returned, and my friend said, "Let's go, sunset is done,"
Now I always have these silent conversations with the Sun, there may be noises but it doesn't really matter now.

The Mask We Wear

It is difficult to realize but truly we all have a mask with us,
We wear it every day and move around,
We see through the mask, and strangely the eyes have filters in them,
We see beauty, not from the natural eye, but through a filter, a camera lens to be precise,
We smile wearing that mask, as the lips also have a fake smile attached to it,
Sometimes the smile is deceptive and strange, like a devil watching on us from hell,
The words that come out are also deceptive, as we say one thing and mean something else,
Although the meaning is never related, it is just to take advantage of someone,
But when we need to curse someone, the real words just come up,

As we leave the true feelings behind, we are filled with rage and that is what we want,
Quietly every day without anyone knowing we wear this face, as it becomes convenient and stress-free,
I believe the only time we had an identity was when we were kids,
That time we didn't think too much about who-said-what,
We were so happy just growing up, simple fights never meant that we'd block others,
All these ideas emerged slowly as we grew up, that is when the world showed a different side,
We have all emotions in this mask, it is so nicely built,
We even cry but it has no feelings, it has tear drops but those are lies,
It's only when someone close to us and the one we rely on hurts us, that we really cry,
I feel suffocated in this mask, don't know why, the world seems to have adapted to the same, why can't I
Well, this question will always be unanswered,
The mask we wear has become a part of us, now and always.

City Lights

The night is filled with stars, but still we need
lights,
As the night slowly comes to heart, there is a
feeling of a building filled with lights,
Every window showcases a different scene all
together,
Everyone in those homes has a different fight,
The struggle they go through is not the same,
some have financial,
Some have distance with their partners, and
some have kids and school troubles,
But behind these close towers and towers
touching the skies,
Every room and balcony has shimmering lights,
As I gaze through my car window, I wonder
what the town will look like,

That is when I decided to drive up the mountain to catch a glimpse at the same time,
Moving past the big poles on the street giving streetlights,
Felt these would be like fruits hanging from a tree from that far but insight,
They enlightened my path like books in school many times, at night when you need them to pave a path,
I was trying to draw a picture with all this in mind, how these street lights will blend with the building's glow,
This was the time when I saw the stadium, it had full flood lights on as they were testing for a match soon,
This was another sight to watch and my drawing of lights was moving on,
Now approaching the mountains, I found that the road was dark, the light closest to me was illuminating the path,
This was my car's headlight which was glowing and telling directions of the path,
Once I parked and left my car lights on, I saw a great vision of a different world, that was fully bright and talking,
Silent conversation happening between the lights,

City lights are blinding and amazing but are a
chatterbox which was feeling inside, that is
when a small light came up,
This was my mobile phone as if it was left out,
Amazing was the beauty together, City lights
you just rock so much.

Depressed but still need to fight

I used to have a happy life, things were different, and I had a smile,
I am not sure when various things came up,
Life took a U-turn, and things just broke up,
I was struggling to see where I was heading this time,
When it was a direct collision with a wall that I didn't see,
It was a depressive feeling overall, I was not sure what to do after all,
Things further derailed when the emotional aspect hit all the time,
Layer after layer, I was finding people's true colors,

Difficult to cope with this stress, now I was depressed,
Fighting a lone battle with myself in the mirror, medication came up but my hands tremor,
To worsen the situation my inner self said bye-bye,
I don't want to be the person you always have been, your character looks real,
But still, you look like a phony, I don't want to play the role of this losing soul,
Come back to me when you are right, now I was in a tunnel with no light,
I kept walking, thinking soon things would change, there is always light in the end,
Still found nothing near, kept falling into anger and rage forever,
Then went back to my old self, asked for suggestions and said it was no movie dear,
It said then why are you behaving like that, why don't you get up and fight,
I started to do that once again, due to darkness fell but didn't give up,
I am still depressed, it is the truth, someday maybe my expectation will fulfill,
That people also want to talk to me sometimes,
It's not just me reaching out, they do as well,
Hope is hope can't think more, loneliness is surely permanent, need to prepare for that, for sure,

I still want to be the nice person who thinks for others, it’s not a phony character it's just me and what I have always been like.

Printed by Libri Plureos GmbH in Hamburg, Germany

9 789363 309647